T0209276

EMBRACING
the HEARTBEAT
of GOD

My Second Book

PASTOR ANNIE S. BLACKWELL

WESTBOW
PRESS®
A DIVISION OF THOMAS NELSON
& ZONDERVAN

WestBow Press books may be ordered through booksellers or by contacting:

WestBow Press
A Division of Thomas Nelson & Zondervan
1663 Liberty Drive
Bloomington, IN 47403
www.westbowpress.com
1 (866) 928-1240

ISBN: 978-1-9736-5541-1 (sc)
ISBN: 978-1-9736-5540-4 (hc)
ISBN: 978-1-9736-5542-8 (e)

Library of Congress Control Number: 2019902488

Print information available on the last page.

WestBow Press rev. date: 04/04/2019

CONTENTS

CHAPTER 1

I'M STARTING ALL OVER AGAIN

E leven years have passed since I was in the hospital for lupus. I've had no flare-ups that have caused me to be admitted to the hospital. I have now been a survivor of SLE lupus for forty years and four months, and I'm now taking two pills instead of eighteen, and those two are a blood thinner and a blood pressure pill.

I praise God for all He has brought me through. Having had to go through terrible side effects was mind-boggling and an awful thing to live with every day. I have had to learn how to walk all over again twice in my struggle with lupus. I had to take therapy after my last flare-up. I have had two strokes, but they told me about only one of them, which happened sometime in 1993 or 1994; the doctor never explained the other one to me.

That stroke happened in 2006 as I woke up one morning and went downstairs; I realized something was wrong with me. I staggered to the stairs. As I stood at the top of the stairs, I began to feel dizzy. The room started swirling around, so I knelt to keep myself from falling down the stairs. I waited for a while before I began to walk downstairs. I felt worse with each step, and there were thirteen of them. I finally made it to the bottom; the room was still spinning around. I was sweaty, and I felt I was passing out. There was no one in the house with me.

I walked around the sides of the walls grasping them until I reached the door that went into the living room. I fell on the sofa, which was near the door. The room was still spinning. I was frightened and did not know what I was going to do. I closed my eyes as tight as I could hoping this feeling would soon go away. But it didn't. It got worse.

I somehow fell asleep again, and as I woke up, my husband was standing in the doorway looking at me. He asked me if I was all right. I could hardly speak; my mouth just twitched as I tried to say something. He was about to go back outside because he was fixing something on the car. He asked me again whether I was all right. I nodded knowing very well that my whole body was feeling terrible. I thought I might feel better if I just tried to rest and take it easy. My head felt as if it would burst open.

I think I took three pain pills, and I somehow fell back to sleep. I was still in the house by myself. All I could do was pray that God would touch my body—that whatever was happening to me would be gone when I woke up. I had the most painful headache going down my neck, but I still wasn't thinking I should get up and go to the ER. I guess I had lain there about half the day before I woke up again. I had to go to the bathroom. I staggered there gripping every wall and calling on the name of Jesus every step.

The room was spinning faster than before, and my headache had gotten worse. I felt pain in my eyes, but I trusted God to touch my body. I never liked going to the hospital; I was trying to tough it out. I hoped my faith would kick in because I wholeheartedly believed in God first.

I took some more pain pills, and before I knew it, I had drifted back to sleep as the room was still spinning even when my eyes were closed. I felt something going around in my body as I became very weak.

At about three, the grandchildren came home from school and saw me on the sofa crying. I asked them where was my husband, and they said he was outside working. I told them to tell him to come in. They went and got him, and when he came in the room, he asked me what was wrong. I told him to get me out of here. He asked whether I wanted to go to the hospital. I said yes because my headache was causing even my eyes and ears to ache. So that is how I ended up in the hospital that day.

My pain was so great that they had to give me a shot of morphine. I felt the pain easing as I drifted off to sleep. I woke up again within two hours because the morphine had worn off; they gave me more in an IV. I prayed to the Lord to help me understand what was going on with me. I had seen the doctor, but he had told me nothing. I ended up in the hospital for nine days. I wasn't able to even get to the bathroom by myself.

All that time, my room was spinning around, and no one told me what was going on with me. I wasn't allowed to get out of bed without being supervised. That is when I realized just how sick I was. I ended up having to make a choice whether to go to the nursing home for a while or go up to the fifth floor of the hospital. They insisted that they weren't going to send me home with my husband. I was just that bad; they felt that he would not be able to take care of me by himself because I could not even sit up in my bed for even a few minutes at a time.

They put a sensor on my bed beneath me. There was one also in the chair beside my bed so in case I tried to get up by myself, they would know it. I kept asking the nurse what was wrong with me; she said I had to wait to ask the doctor the questions, but he never came. I guessed he looked at my chart at the nurses' station and told the nurses what to do. I felt he was trying to avoid talking to me about my situation. I don't know what he had discussed with my husband and children, but I know he kept avoiding me. Maybe he didn't want to tell me the whole truth fearing I might not know how to accept it.

I ended up walking with a walker before I left the hospital. I couldn't believe this was happening to me again. I was unable to walk by myself, and I was still under the influence of the medications when I was discharged. I didn't go anywhere but to my appointments for my therapy during that hospital stay. I thought

I would never walk again; I couldn't even stand up by myself. The room spun whether I was sitting up or lying down, whether my eyes were open or closed.

But God brought me through. I have always been a strong believer in God; having faith in Him has elevated my belief even more. Jesus and I got our own thing going on! My faith is what has brought me this far, and it is what I have been trusting and leaning on. I thank my God that He walked with me through it all including my ignorance of not going to the hospital when I should have gone. It's all because of my true relationship with God. That made the difference as I struggled with lupus as well as other things that came up in my life.

On September 12, 2013, God called me into the ministry as a pastor. How ironic it was because I had been saved on September 12, 1965. At first, I was a little afraid about even accepting that calling, but I knew God was calling me. Many things have happened to me, but I never doubted God was there for me. I was a little shaky in my body, yes, but I never lost my faith in God though at times I became uncomfortable waiting on Him. All I had been through positioned me to where I am in God now.

I have always wanted to be as close to God as I could get. I have always served Him with my whole heart, body, soul, and mind. Though I had stumbled and failed, with God, I got back up. My God is a God of many chances, not just second chances. As I wrote in my first book, "It was only by God's grace and mercy ..."

I had allowed Satan to deceive me after my first husband passed. I detoured from the right path for just a season because I allowed myself to become angry with God and everybody else. Some whom I thought would be there for me had mistreated me. You will never understand my praise for God unless you have read my first book. You will understand how I've been through a lot but the Lord was always with me. He walked me through all I had to go through though I didn't understand why things had happened to me as they had from my childhood on. It wasn't until I got my thoughts and feelings in the right position that I realized God's grace and mercy had kept me; He walked with me through every season of my life.

I didn't really understand a thing about God until I had been married four months after I turned seventeen; that was when I got weak and had no strength of my own to cope with life at my level of faith. I did not know God as my personal Savior then. God told His grace to walk with me and His mercy to pick me up and carry me, and they both have stayed with me to this day. I thank God for His grace and mercy even when I didn't understand what was going on in my life and why it was happening.

I now count my life all joy because He had been there for me at all times. I delight in serving the Lord after having going through all I have. I am still after the heartbeat of God. My failures and shortcomings have never made me stop seeking God's face. I thank God because of that zeal to seek Him when I first gave Him my heart that He had given me. It has never left me though I slipped and fell from grace for a short while.

When I first gave my heart to Him at age seventeen, I didn't understand what had happened to me, but I just let Him have His way with me even when I got angry with Him. I later realized that was a dangerous thing to do even though it was because of my ignorance as I grappled with sickness and the death of my first husband.

After twenty-three years of marriage, I had to start my life over without him. I was devastated and miserable. I asked, "Why me, Lord?" The Spirit answered, "Why not you? You aren't the first widow, and you won't be the last." I was angry, but my soul still longed for God's touch. I just didn't know how to reach out to God out of my devastation at that time. I felt alone; God seemed nowhere to be found. I tried to regroup in that trying time but didn't know how; I felt like I was in another world, a strange place. I had never been to this place with someone who was so close to my heart.

I had to learn how to start living again without my husband of twenty-three years. Being alone was something new to me. I constantly repented and felt sorrowful for my ignorance about God. Losing a spouse is devastating when husband and wife had been so devoted to each other. I didn't know that God would bless me with someone I would start my life over with. I started letting my true feelings and desires come back to my heart. Though I went through that period of hurt with a wounded heart and anger, I still desired to go after God's heart. I knew He was still moving in my life and was still with me. Yes, a lot still happened to me in the eight and a half years I was single because I let my fear take hold of me and I was afraid of almost everybody who wanted to get close to me. I fought to keep my sanity.

When my current husband and I were married on June 7, 1997, God start moving me into another dimension of my life. I became a member of my husband's denomination.

Remaining Steadfast in Holiness

I had been brought up in holiness; it was embedded in my soul, mind, body, spirit, and heart. I sincerely desired to follow God. I was not thought of too well because I had gone to another church, but I knew God had placed me there with my second husband. Others didn't realize that it didn't matter which church I attended; I would always try to live a holy and righteous life wherever I was because I knew who I was in God and to whom I belonged. No denomination could get me to stray from God's Word. I knew from my reading what sound doctrine was. I had always known that my salvation was not in a church's name but in the way I lived—a holy lifestyle before God. The apostle Paul warned Timothy that holiness was the key to living a righteous lifestyle before God.

The first Sunday after we were married, we stepped into that church and were greeted by some of the members. We decided to go by the Lord's leading when we made our marriage plans. Ours wasn't a big wedding, though that was what I had wanted. I realized God had not planned that for me.

As I stepped into that church that morning, the Spirit said to me, "This is not your destiny either. You are here only for a season." I began to ponder His words. I wondered how long God's season for me would be and when I would know it was time to leave.

I wasn't there just because I had married a man from that denomination. It was much deeper than that; God had destined me to be there even before I was born. God began to show me some things that had been going on and were still going on. I had entered an atmosphere different from what I had been used to, but things began to happen while I was there. God began to show me the demons who were coming after me. He showed me some people who were already against me though they didn't know me. They began to harm and hurt me secretly. I had to learn how to handle them with care and still love them. As things began to unfold, I tried to be friendly and comfortable there.

Standing Steadfast in My Faith

My faith and belief were being tested, but I held onto my faith and belief in God as I had learned to do from the Word. I held on to fasting and praying. I didn't try to adapt to the church; I concentrated on being a true, faithful, and committed Christian who was simply in a different atmosphere. I knew who I was in God. I stayed away from some people because of their attitudes and feelings for me; I didn't worry about their spirits because God was on my side and was with me. Denominations didn't matter to me because I had learned from scripture.

Over thirty-two years previously, I had vowed to God that I would accept the Bible and practice its teachings rightly dividing the word of truth and abiding in it the best I could. We should all do that. "Nevertheless, whereto we have already attained, let us walk by the same rule, let us mind the same thing" (Philippians 3:16 KJV).

I had to change the way I worshipped the Lord, but I held onto my spiritual integrity. I wasn't ashamed about how the Spirit would fall on me; I didn't quench the Spirit when He would fall on me. It wasn't about how I worshipped; it was all about what was in my heart. Worshipping Him in spirit and in truth is the key to it all.

Well, it got to the point that some people were offended by the way I was worshipping God because I would give myself right to the Spirit and worship God in my own way. The Spirit always warned me beforehand when I was going to be attacked by some people for how I praised God and yielded my will to the Spirit. I would let the Lord have His way with me. I wasn't used to sitting still and quenching the Spirit of the Lord. If nobody else would praise Him, I would. Some said that it didn't take all that, but I held onto my faith and belief in God and my way of worshipping Him because I knew it took that and more to please Him, and I wasn't ashamed to praise God my way with radical praise. I established my faith in God for my own good. He was taking me where He wanted to, and I was letting Him do that!

That was definitely worshipping God sincerely in spirit and in truth, and I didn't let anyone change me in that regard. I did not fit comfortably where I was, but I focused on Jesus. I wondered if this was a test of my faith, but I never lost my praise or my hope and faith in Jesus Christ though I felt like a square trying to fit into a circle.

Sometimes when the Spirit would fall on me, I would see some squirming and quenching the Spirit. Maybe it was because some didn't understand how the Spirit would move among us as I was used to letting Him move me. When I would preach, some would say they liked other preachers because they didn't preach as long as I did. Some were always in a hurry to leave church; it seemed church wasn't that important to them. I would just smile and walk away. I didn't feel good about that, but I didn't let it intimidate me or change my way of praising God. I thought they weren't really sincere in their relationship with God. I tossed their complaints over my shoulder and kept on praying to God, who kept telling me, "It's only for a season."

I faithfully and happily served God in that church in every area and position I was led to serve in, and I loved what I was doing in the

Lord. My brother was a janitor at that church; after he left it, I took on his job secretly, and nobody knew who was keeping the church clean. I always found something to do in the church and didn't look to be paid for doing it because I loved the Lord.

I served that church as a Sunday school superintendent and secretary and on the mission board. I taught adult, youth, and children Sunday school, and I was the choir director for a while. I served on the usher board and the kitchen committee and as a devotion or worship leader. I was also one of the band leaders; they along with the pastor were each responsible for ten church members' spiritual growth. Band leaders checked on them if they missed church too often; they visited them to see if they had any problems the church could help them with. Band leaders gave reports every quarter about how their members were doing spiritually.

That was all new to me as I was in a different denomination that worshipped God differently. I saw hate and felt envy and strife among some because I would let go and let God have His way with me and praise Him my way by shouting and dancing. I kept asking God, "How long, Lord, will I have to stay here?" I had a choice about where my husband and I would worship. I respected my husband and didn't want to uproot him from his church, where he was a licensed deacon even though I was a licensed minister in my church. We had agreed to go to his church because I would not allow our house to be divided. We were two in the flesh but one in the Spirit, and I was loving it! I realize now that God wanted to teach me something else about worshipping Him in a different atmosphere.

Getting Acquainted with the Saints

I was accepted by some and envied by others. I was also hated by some for no reason, which was nothing new according to God's Word. He kept me strong in the midst of it all. That was one reason I started having noonday prayer by myself at home. I found ways to stay strong in the Lord and in His presence. When I learned that deacons had keys to the church, I used my husband's key to get into the church every day at noon so I could sit in God's presence and talk to Him. Sometimes, I would pray to Him for an hour or more as time would sometimes slip by. That has always been my dedication any time of the day when I prayed to God.

I sometimes went to the church in the evening and fell on my knees with nothing to say as my tears flowed. Sometimes, I didn't know how to come before Him in those hard times as I tried to keep my sanity. I felt trapped in a place I didn't want to be any longer. But I knew God was interpreting my hurt and tears, so I would have conversations with the Lord as if He were sitting right beside me. In fact, He was; I could feel His presence.

I found a way to keep my faith increasing and strong in the Lord. Sometimes, all I could do was just sit there before God and the Spirit would fall on me all of a sudden. That was when my heart was heavy and overwhelmed by hurt. I began to pray in tongues, and some in our congregation were opposed to that during services because they didn't understand anything about speaking in tongues. God would sometimes give me the interpretation of it, but some didn't want to accept that.

Jesus and I would have conversations. Once, I had to ask God to forgive me whenever the Spirit would fall on me. At times, I quenched the Spirit because of how some would react to that. I knew God was not pleased with me for doing that, so when my spirit was troubled, I didn't know how to pray to God or what to say to Him.

However, I knew God was able to interpret the unknown tongues I was uttering, so noonday prayer was where my strength was—alone with Him. During my noonday prayer, I just let go and let God have His way with me the way He always did. I could pray in tongues as long as I wanted to, and God would interpret it for me; He would talk to me in the Spirit. I was determined not to fail God or fall again! It didn't matter how I was treated; I knew where I could go for strength and relief. My favorite secret places were in church alone or in my bedroom. I didn't want to quench the Spirit again even if that meant praying alone.

God had placed me in that church for a purpose, reason, and season. For thirty-two years, I had been surrounded by people I was familiar with—family and others—and we fellowshipped in our worship. They praised the Lord as I believed we should praise Him. We didn't have programs, protocols, or time limits at our services. Nobody was in a hurry to leave; they wanted to be there when the Spirit would take over and move them. Our pastor told us that those who ever wanted to leave were free to do so, but a remnant always stayed until the end of the service.

I experienced some rough spots there, but God invited me to a higher level in my walk with Him. He helped me understand that what came with bigger churches were bigger devils I had to learn to face. I would have to conquer giants in my walk with Him through my faith in Him. He wanted me to understand that I would achieve that higher level and become stronger in Him by fasting and prayer. Matthew 17:21 (KJV) reads, "Howbeit this kind goeth not out but by fasting and prayer." He was getting ready to elevate me, but my heart would actually ache and long for where I had come from.

Sometimes when I was in the pulpit, I felt my heart crying for the church and the Spirit of the Lord I had felt for thirty-two years in a place that I had felt established and comfortable, a place I knew I could always go back to if I chose. But God's plan for me was never to go backward; it was to always press forward. I kept on hearing God say, "It's only for a season."

I learned to fight and survive even in the midst of my enemies. I learned to engage in spiritual warfare with the enemy without fear. We can claim to have a lot of faith, but our faith will be tested in life's battles, and we won't know how much faith we have until it has been tested. My prayers and fasting became my weapons against the giants and the familiar spirits who had taken over the church.

The Lord showed me some of the strongholds that had arisen in the church. It seems that the majority of people there went along with whatever happened whether it was right or wrong because they wasn't strong in the Lord. But God allowed me to see what was happening in that church, and that made me more determined than ever to press on that much harder while holding onto my integrity and steadfastness, which my former pastor had preached and embedded in my soul and heart.

CHAPTER 2

THE SIGN GOD SHOWED ME IN THE CHURCH

After I was at that church for thirteen long years, I saw that the glory of the Lord was about to be lifted out of it. It seemed that very few recognized what was happening and would happen because few were heeding what was being preached or how the Word was warning them repeatedly. Some had no fear about speaking against God's preached Word. They did not fear God or men or women of God; they would just speak out while the pastor preached. I felt it was getting close to the time for us to leave; I feared being there after seeing the last thing God showed me.

As I was sitting in the pulpit one Sunday morning waiting for the service to start, I had my head down trying to become consecrated. I lifted my head to see how full the church was. There it was—a sign on the wall, proof that God was about to bring judgment. I couldn't believe what I was seeing, so I closed my eyes and shook my head hoping I hadn't seen what I thought I had seen. But when I opened my eyes, I saw it again. I could not get into service that morning. It left me speechless, and I couldn't tell anyone what I had seen. I felt a grieving spirit come over me. I sat as the service was going on; I was there in body only. The sign disappeared after a while, but the fear of God was on me so heavily that morning.

During the service, the Spirit began to move heavily; a weeping spirit came over the church. Different people began to cry out. The Spirit got higher and sat in the midst of the service. A spirit of conviction swept through the church. Some begin to cry out; others were crying and couldn't stop. God said to me, "It's not a rejoicing spirit but a repentant spirit crying out!"

As the spirit of conviction moved through the church, different people began to cry out as God called them to repentance, but they seemed not to understand what was happening. No one left his or her seat. The Lord had visited us that morning very forcefully; the Spirit was moving heavily.

I caught the eye of a friend, the chairman of the deacon board, who looked at me with eyes that said he was trying to figure out what was going on with me. He noticed I wasn't getting into the service as I usually did. I had begun to cry and couldn't stop.

After the benediction, he came over to me and asked, "What's going on with you?" I tried to smile and look him in the eye, but I couldn't. I asked, "What do you mean?" though I knew what he meant. He said, "I watched you during the whole service, and you weren't here with us. You were somewhere else." I started to tell him what the Lord had shown me, what I had seen, but I couldn't talk about it. All I could say to him was, "I'm all right." My friend is full of the Spirit. I have seen God use him many times to warn the church, but they ignored whatever he said.

Not long after, the same feeling came over me in another service. I knew for sure it was time for us to go. They had been warned many times, but they failed to accept the warnings. Some talked and made mockery of the preaching and the preacher because it hadn't come from whom they wanted it to come. The warning was a big joke to them.

It had been thirteen years since we had gotten married, but it was time for us to leave the church.

Stepping Out in Faith

Yes, we were criticized and questioned by some about why we were leaving, but it was not for me to try to explain why we were leaving to anyone but the pastor. I had told him it was time for us to go, and he didn't question me. He said, "If God has told you to go, that's what y'all have to do. Obey Him. But whatever you do or wherever you go, never build your church on the choir or anything else but the Bible. Whatever you do, let God lead you."

He gave us his blessings, and that was enough confirmation for me. I had thought he wouldn't understand my reasons for leaving. The devil made me believe he would give me the third degree for even leaving and taking one of his members (smile). Even if he had, I would have told him what God had told me to say. But he understood exactly what we had to do. My husband and I had talked about it. I had given him the option of staying without me—I would understand that—but I was going to obey God.

He said, "We're married. I'll go where you go because you and I are one. I knew you were a minister before I became involved with you, and I knew that the time would come when you would have to leave this church. I knew what I was getting myself into because the Lord had already showed me this. I will never stand in your way of what God tells you to do. I knew you were not a speaker but a preacher of the Word."

I thought my hindrances to worshipping God as I desired had left. We started visiting another church, but the same words kept coming back: "This is not your destiny either." God was sending me out to start from scratch and depend completely on Him, but I wanted to hook up with another church for a while.

I tried to stay and help build that church up. We painted and cleaned the church and made it beautiful. I hemmed and hung curtains on the windows. Our colors were gold and white because that was what was in my heart; gold represented the kingship of God and white represented the purity of His presence there. I did as God had instructed me to do.

We worked faithfully as if we were already members of the church. They hadn't taken us in as members yet, but we went there faithfully every service anyhow. The church went from five of us to seven of us in about a month. People started coming and visiting the church. Then a confrontation rose and the truth came out. We had been fooled into thinking that maybe soon or later on we would become members of the church. We walked up on them talking one Sunday morning as we were coming in the church, and they stopped their conversation when they saw us. I thought God was sending me there and I might become the pastor of that church. I thought that was God's will for me, but it wasn't.

One member told that they might let me be the pastor five or some years down the road. That was after we had fixed up the church. "Y'all don't believe like we do anyway, so let us go our different ways," I said. God wouldn't let me feel hurt or discouraged. I heard Him say, "This is not your destiny either." I had to repent for moving as I desired to move. God had not been in that move at all.

God was going to show us where to go, but I had chosen in the beginning to let man decided for me where to get started. We didn't hesitate to leave when an uncomfortable spirit of division rose up in the church one Sunday morning. God showed us it wasn't the place He had sent us to.

We shook the dust from our feet. It says in Matthew 10:14 (KJV), "And whosoever shall not receive you, nor hear your words, when ye depart out of that house or city, shake off the dust of your feet." We knew we were not welcome there anymore. We had tithed to the church, but they would never let us attend any meetings. The church had only three members before we got there. We didn't know what they were doing with our money or what was really going on in the church. I'd ask about having a meeting, but they would always say, "We already had a meeting."

We never looked back, and we don't regret leaving. We didn't regret doing what we had done in that church because we knew that God would bless us for that and that He had greater things for us.

Still Seeking Guidance from God

A few weeks later, a pastor asked me to help her at her church, so we started going there regularly. I didn't want to because it had never entered my spirit or heart to join there and I hadn't heard from God on it. We went there, but I felt it was not the direction God was leading me. I had a holy way of worship embedded in me in a holiness church, and any other kind of worship would not be right for me. I felt I was going backward in my worship of God because their worship was totally different from mine. I sometimes felt the Spirit of God there, but I wasn't used to being programmed in worship and praise. I couldn't adapt to that way of worship. I was used to the Spirit coming into our midst and not worrying about protocol or the length of the service. I was used to letting the Lord have His way with me and just yield to the Spirit. I knew who I was in God and what I desired from His Word. I knew what I was looking for—a higher height and a deeper depth in my relationship with God. I was seeking His heart, wisdom, knowledge, and understanding of His Word because my soul was not satisfied with where I had been or by what had happened to us.

I was hungry and thirsty for God; I was not satisfied with where we were. God's full glory was missing from the service there; the Spirit was never fully allowed to manifest Himself to the people. It seemed they were afraid to let go and let the Spirit have His way with them. I was used to seeing the Lord manifesting Himself to His people freely. I'm not talking about dancing in the Spirit all the time, but I have seen the glory of the Lord come into services like a fog and slay worshippers in the Spirit throughout the church. People would get up and run to the altar crying out to God for salvation. I had witnessed that many times, but I did not ask God why this was happening to us that way.

I thought leaving there would go easily and smoothly, but that did not happen. I knew I had to still trust God because I knew what I had heard God say to me. Yes, by that time, I had become discouraged and afraid, but I was sure what I had heard at noonday prayer that day. The enemy had told me that God hadn't called me to be a pastor, and that prompted me to ask, "Lord, is this your will for us to be here? If it's not, it will be okay with me."

The whole time we were there, I questioned God about it, but my husband was uncomfortable with not having a leader's covering over us. I had followed him with his decision to join that church, but just as soon as we had, I heard, "This is not your destiny either." I felt I was going backward in the Lord because I was more advanced in the Word than that church was.

It wasn't that I felt better than everybody else; I just knew what God had placed in me. I knew in my heart that there was a higher height and deeper depth in God I was searching for. I'm not talking about a higher position but more of God manifesting Himself in my life. As it says in the Bible, signs follow believers. I wanted the works of Jesus to be manifest in our lives as it happened when Jesus walked on the earth. That was what I was after because I believed the Bible totally.

I take God at His Word and I want to see His Word manifested in my life for real, not just dress up, go to church, and sit in a pew. I do not want to be a programmed worshipper. I want to get into God's presence for real. I need to be where I can seek God's face the way my heart drives me to do. I want to go after God even at home. I have a deep longing for God that pushes me to go after God with my whole being.

I felt I had wasted too much time. I wanted to feel God's presence in church and be strengthened by that. I felt that God wanted to equip me for better and greater things to happen in my life for His glory. I felt I had been put back into a growing mold seeking the knowledge of God. So we gave the tithes we were holding onto to that church. We had been saving our tithes and offerings though we gave other money to the churches we visited. Twice we had sown seeds into churches, but after we had joined that church, we decided to give the tithes we had saved to it. I did it, but I wasn't led by God to do it. I just thought it was the proper thing to do because we had joined that church.

Every now and then, it would bother me in my spirit. By that time, I had started attending women's conferences again. It had been about fourteen years since I had last been to one because where I had been, the women didn't seem to be interested in going to things like that. But I wanted to seek out ways to get closer to God and grow stronger in Him because I have never been satisfied with where I was in the Lord. According to the Word, there is more to God than meets the eye.

Seeking God's Will for My Life

At the conference, I took a class led by a prophetess. She was led to pray for each one of her students. We stood in line before we left for lunch, and she prophesied to some of us as she prayed. As the line got shorter, I began to feel fear. The closer I got to her, the more I felt the fear of the Lord increasing in me. When I stood in front of her, she said, "I have only three words from the Lord for you: 'It is finished.'"

I left her class confused, ashamed, and afraid because she had spoken to me in the presence of the other students. I couldn't sleep that night because all I could think about was those three words. Jesus had said those three words when He was crucified: "When Jesus therefore had received the vinegar, he said, 'It is finished,' and he bowed his head and gave up the ghost" (John 19:30 KJV). I asked God that night, "Lord, am I going to die? Is it really over for me? What's going to happen to me? Lord, let me see that woman again in the morning!" The next morning was the last day of the conference; I needed to know the meaning of those three words for me. I was full of fear and restless all night long; my imagination was running wild. I didn't want to go home feeling as I did.

The next morning, I went to morning devotion and looked for the woman. I didn't really remember what she looked like, but I remembered the young woman who had been carrying her books for her. I had given her a note to give to the prophetess the previous night to let her know I needed to talk with her.

Devotion was almost over, but still no prophetess. After the benediction, I rushed to the door and out into the hallway; there she was talking to someone. I walked up so she could see me. I wanted to talk to her before I went to my other class. After she finished talking to the young woman, I asked her if she had gotten my note. She said, "Yes, and I was hoping I'd see you again."

My Purpose Began to Unfolded

She boldly asked me, "When will you do what the Lord has told you to do? I don't know where you are going to church now, but you don't belong there. That is not your destiny. You were supposed to been had your church. What are you waiting for?"

All I could say was, "I'm waiting on the Lord." I knew she was speaking prophetic words to me; that wasn't the first time someone had spoken those words to me, and that wasn't the first time I had said, "I'm waiting on the Lord." I was afraid to walk out on my faith in my calling. I didn't even know how to begin to go forth.

She said, "No, honey, the Lord is waiting on you. Don't you know that delayed obedience is disobedience?"

I explained what I had done—given over $2,000 in tithes we had saved up to the church we had just joined after my husband had become weary about not having a covering over us.

"You were not supposed to give that money away," she said. "It was for you to start your own church. But don't worry about it. God will make provision for you again. This time, don't give it away."

I left that conference with the fear of God all over me. I thought about what the prophetess had told me and where I was to go from there and how to get started. I was afraid, but I knew she hadn't lied to me because God had been dealing with me already for a while. That's one reason I was having noonday prayer at home.

The next Sunday as I sat in that chair up in that pulpit, I began to praise the Lord when the music and the choir started up. I was trying to shake off the feeling that had risen in me. I felt I was really out of place and disconnected from God. I heard a demanding voice say, "Sit down. This is not your destiny!"

CHAPTER 3

FEAR OF THE LORD GRIPPED MY HEART

I was convicted of what the prophetess had told me. I didn't feel right in my spirit sitting in that pulpit. The feeling that had come over me wouldn't leave; it made me restless in everything I tried to do. It was heavy on me. But I realized we had to leave that church too. I had to call the pastor and say we needed to talk with her the next Sunday. I didn't know how I would break the news to her, but the fear of God was tearing me up.

As usual, we were the first ones to get to church. We sat in our car waiting for the pastor; I wondered how I would break the news to her and where I would go from there. I was afraid to step out by myself and to fail God by not doing as well as other pastors had. They seemed to be doing so well and prospering as pastors. I was letting my imagination take control of my thinking. I was wondering if I would ever pastor in a way that would please God.

The pastor drove up. I became tense about what I had to say to her, and I feared what she would say to me. As we were going into the church, I didn't know what to say. I dreaded every step we took to her office. We sat, and she smiled at us as usual. She asked, "What did you want to talk to me about?"

I quickly said, "We're asking for your blessings because we have to leave the church." That was all God had me to say.

She sat there silently for a moment. Her countenance fell. "Okay, you have my blessings. But why are you leaving?"

All I could say was that it was time for us to leave. I couldn't explain our decision in greater detail because we simply didn't know where we was going; all I knew was that it was time for us to go even though we had just joined that church. It just wasn't in God's will for us to stay there. I felt I had detoured from God's will for my life. I had become uncomfortable sitting in the pulpit. The Spirit had begun convicting me of what the prophetess had told me. Every word she had spoken to me had stayed in my spirit; I couldn't shake them. I knew what God had told me the moment we went to that church, but I had tried to keep it pushed into the back of my mind. I wanted to be nice and respectful to the pastor. God hadn't sent me there; I had gone there myself just to be nice. God made that known to that prophetess, and I had to get back on track with God's directions.

After leaving that church, my husband and I agreed that we would visit churches but never get trapped into joining another church. I had to do what God had called me to do years before. I knew I had been running from my call. I had thought someone would give me a place that was already set up. How wrong I had been; it didn't come that easily. Yes, I would take appointments and preach, but I never let it be known that God was dealing with me about pastoring a church because I didn't desire to do that and was scared to do that. I didn't know how to do it, and that was messing my mind up. I was afraid to accept such a positon because I had seen my former pastor crying before his members. I had worked in the church very closely with him, and God had allowed me to feel his burden many times.

I had often seen him standing in front of the congregation broken down and crying for the souls under him who had rebelled against him. Many times, we had visited him. He would show me some of his old books. I enjoyed hanging at his house with him. I hadn't realized it then, but I was seeking for the depths of God way back then. I had a passion for reading and studying God's Word.

The Lord had given me the gift of prophecy and the spirit of discernment, but I became afraid of some of God's gifts; I didn't understand that, and I would ask my pastor about what the Spirit had been showing me. I was young in the Lord, and sometimes, the Lord allowed me to feel his pain as he stood crying before the church begging them to live right as best they could.

I was very close to my pastor because he taught me a lot about being faithful to God. I used to read the scriptures for him as he would preach. But the enemy had belittled me so much that I pondered it in my heart with no intentions to go any further with that one. I had seen that my pastor had had to deal with disobedient people. I always wanted to sing and lead devotion, but I never wanted to become a pastor in anyone's church. That wasn't God's plan for me; He had a far better purpose, plan, reason, and destiny for me, and He would not let me rest until I said yes to Him.

God was requiring a complete surrender of my life to Him when I first was saved. I didn't understand what was taking place in my life back then because I was only seventeen and didn't understand the Word of God as I do now. If nobody else understood why I had to go and do what I had to do my way, I certainly did. I had to decide whether to obey God or live in fear because I had not obeyed Him.

Moving Forward Not by Sight but by Faith

We visited other churches, but I never felt completely comfortable there because I kept hearing, "This is not your destiny either." God was making sure I wouldn't settle for less than what He had planned for me. He told me, "Observe all things." I had become a little discouraged because of what I had seen in some of those churches. I didn't have a desire to continue being with them. God knew I was not satisfied going from church to church every Sunday morning, so He told me, "Start having church in your home until I tell you what to do." I spoke to some of my family members who were not attending church; I did not want to draw anyone away from the church he or she was attending. I was willing to wait on the Lord, and this time for sure. So I started having church in my dining room.

It was just my husband and I for the first few services. I felt out of place because there was no crowd around me there, but I was satisfied doing what I knew I was supposed to do. My spirit pressed me to do it. I told myself, *Don't expect a crowd of people. Just obey God's voice.*

We would get up and get ready for church as if we were going out to church. We started in March 2010 in my dining room. We would take up our little offerings as if the room were full, and it always felt it was. We even start sacrificing and putting a little bit more in the offering. I felt content in what I was doing and how I was going about it; my soul was satisfied in the Lord! I felt good about just obeying God.

I kept on praying to the Lord and doing what I felt in my heart was right to do. Then a few of my family members started coming, and they seemed excited about it. We would start our Sunday school service at nine though we didn't have any Sunday school books. I taught from the Bible, and then we started our morning service at eleven, which lasted until twelve or twelve thirty at that latest. Sometimes, the Spirit was in our midst, and that encouraged me to forget about the time and just yield to the Spirit.

I wanted to encourage them to keep coming, so to show my appreciation to them because they could have gone somewhere else to worship, I started cooking dinner for everybody. I would get up at five and cook dinner so they didn't have to go home and cook after service.

Things began to come together; our little services felt like church. We started with five faithful family members, and the Spirit reminded me that the number five represented grace in the Bible; I felt God had set His grace on us and assured us just as He had Moses that He was with us. That was enough encouragement for me to keep on.

Our offerings increased from $5 or $10 to $20 or $30. We were getting excited about serving God at our little home church. We always started on time just as if we had had a building. Yes, we would visit other churches sometimes for afternoon services, but we didn't forget our offerings for our services. Our church hadn't quite been established, but we praised God faithfully for what He was doing and would do. The Spirit of the Lord was always there with us and would manifest Himself in that dining room as if we were in a big church!

We held those services in my dining room for two years and nine months. We would always gather expecting the Holy Spirit to be in our midst. I was depending on God's approval every time we met. I looked for God to back me up with His presence. My oldest daughter wanted to attend our services, so she did and started tithing. I can't say she wasn't led to do it, but I know God had His hand in it all. Our offerings begin to increase and especially around income tax time. Jobs got better, and our tithes and offerings increased!

Little Is Much if God's Righteousness Is in It

God was letting me see how He could use just five people; He made provision for His people and church. We had no bank account, but in those two years and nine months, we saved up $50,000. We wanted to open a bank account, but because we didn't have a building or an EIN (a tax ID number), the bank wouldn't let us deposit our tithes and offerings in an account. That, however, didn't discourage or stop us; we kept right on having our services and doing business as usual.

My mother used to tell me when we had just a little bit of food in the house, "Little is much if God is in it." I found that scripture in Proverbs 15:16 and Proverbs 16:8 (KJV): "Better is little with the fear of the Lord than greater treasure and trouble" and "Better is a little with righteousness than great revenues without right." The old saints may not have known how to read the Bible very well, but they said things in the Bible that applied to me. I didn't understand many things my mom told me until I was saved and started studying the Bible.

I became afraid of keeping that much money at home, but that was when God told me, "Look for a building," so we did. We had made large donations to two churches; we always came together faithfully, and we gave our tithes and little offerings faithfully as well. I guess God saw that I was about to make the same mistake again—giving away His money for His church. I realized that our donations to those churches were good deeds but not what God wanted us to do just then.

God kept on blessing us; His hand was on us. We looked at three buildings that we were promised we could rent, but each time, they were rented to someone else who perhaps offered more than the $1,200 in rent we were offering. Nonetheless, I wasn't disappointed because I was doing what God had asked me to do—looking for a building. I said, "Lord, I'm going to try one more time. If that falls through, I won't look any more." Just listen to me telling God what I was going to do. I had gotten in trouble doing that before. I thought about giving the money to a church that I would join, but that was just me talking crazy at that moment. I knew God didn't move when we wanted Him to move; I knew He moved in His own time. I couldn't get out of my head what God had told me to do, and I knew I would never be satisfied in my spirit if I didn't obey Him and reach the place He had for me.

God was not going to let us get just any kind of building. My son started helping me look for a decent place though he was attending another church. About three months later, right when I was about to give up, he told me he had found a building in the next town. He said he had been inside; he said it needed some work.

My heart leaped for joy; at last, we were going to have a building to have church in! I rushed to that town and realized I had passed that building many times but had never noticed it or knew it was vacant. It had been a furniture store. It looked a little too expensive for me, but I loved the looks of it from the outside. I had to remind myself that this wasn't about what I thought but about what God wanted me to have.

I Was Led by the Spirit

I walked into the building and was puzzled. Every wall had been cut off about two-thirds of the way up, and I could see all the way to the back. My heart dropped. I started to walk back to my car, but the landlord and my son came around the end of the hall. The landlord had a pleasant attitude and voice. He asked me to look around. I did, but all I could think was, *I'm not going to spend our money fixing up this building. We just want to rent it. What if something goes wrong and we have to move out?*

I knew that was the enemy trying to suppress my hopeful thoughts. The landlord asked me how I liked it, and all I could think about was how much it would cost us to fix it up. I thought, *Lord, is this really the building for us?*

But then, the landlord said, "If you want it, you can have it. I'll give you four months' free rent if you fix the place up."

I looked at my son; I didn't say anything because I wanted to make sure that God would approve of this. All of a sudden, my son told the man, "We'll take it."

I was wondering who would fix the walls; I was listening for God's voice. And there was my son acting as if he were the head of our church and knew how to fix walls. I didn't know how to do that either. But my son said again, "We'll take it."

I was trying to get his attention to let him know I didn't want it. I asked him, "Who can you get to help do this kind of work?" I purposefully said "you" instead of "we," but he said, "I can do it, Mom!" He was excited for me when I wasn't at all excited for me.

"When have you ever done this type of work?" I asked him, and he said, "I've done this kind of work before. I helped build the hotel that's in Rehobeth Beach. I know how to nail drywall. That's easy to do."

I had nothing else to say but "Yeah, we'll take it." I was thinking, *Lord, how is this building going to turn out when we get finished with it?* I didn't want a jacked-up place or to waste our money. Then I heard the Spirit say, "Don't look at what it look like now. Visualize the finished product." My vision was a little distorted at that moment, but my faith kicked in. I decided to trust God. I rented the building because I was reminded of what God had said to me in 2006 on the day I was to be discharged from the hospital.

On that Wednesday morning at exactly 4:20, I was awakened by the Spirit, who said to me, "As a negative goes into a dark room to develop into a photograph, so will I do with your life. No one will see your negative, just your positive, when I am finished with you. Your life will speak for itself with all my glory showing up."

I signed the lease on April 19, 2013, and every day, my little congregation worked hard and faithfully. We had eleven rooms and two halls that needed drywall. We had to put carpet in what we would use as the sanctuary.

I had been working at a center as a volunteer, and I loved meeting new people. I helped pass out food and clothing to those in need of them. I had worked at a funeral home for ten years, and I loved that work and the people there as well; they were my family away from my own family. But I had to turn my back on all of that because

I had to do what God had called me to do. I spoke aloud without hesitating what I heard God say to me.

I told my son that I wanted the building finished by the last week of June for our first service. So that didn't give us but a couple of months to finish, but God let it happen for us on time, and He even gave us the colors to decorate our church with: gold to represent His glory, white to represent His purity, and purple to represent His royalty and kingship.

We had our first service on Sunday, June 29, 2013. On September 12, 2013, I was installed as the pastor of the New Church of Deliverance. "So built we the wall; and all the wall was joined together unto the half thereof for the people had a mind to work" (Nehemiah 4:6 KJV).

CHAPTER 4

GOD APPROVED
OUR BUILDING

I was content; I could do as God had instructed me where I was supposed to be with His assurance. My destiny had begun, and another level of my walk with God had begun.

A year and a month after we had been there, we had our first Mother's Day service, and we were worshipping and praising the Lord to the highest. It seemed that God's glory had stepped into our midst and overshadowed our service, so we yielded to His spirit and let Him have His way. God poured His glory on us, and His Spirit overwhelmed us.

God began working on the outside as well. A storm came up, and we heard rain beating hard on the tin roof going from front to back and then to the front again, and it stopped as suddenly as it had started. We looked at each other smiling and praising God. The Spirit told me, "God has set His approval on what you have done with this building."

After the service, we went outside and couldn't believe what we saw. It had rained nowhere but on our church! Not even the road in front of the church was wet. That was amazing. Later that day, I asked a young woman if it had rained on her church, and she said it had not. I knew the rain was a sign from God that He was pleased with our service. We didn't have many members, but I could declare that the Spirit and the glory of God rested in our church.

People from other churches visit us now and then and say they can feel the Spirit when they enter our church. They say it feels different from other churches, and they know it is the Spirit they feel. But all the glory belongs to God!

Going after God with My Whole Heart

God didn't stop there; He knew my heart and my desires toward Him. He had given me the name of our church, the New Church of Deliverance, on September 12, 2013, as I was studying the Word. I had been saved at age seventeen on September 12, 1965.

We later joined in fellowship with four other churches; that was the first conference our church took part in. In the latter part of September 2014, I was at that conference listening to the preacher when all of a sudden I felt that the Spirit had put me in a trance. My body was sitting there, but God had taken me in the Spirit above the service. He said in a soft but demanding voice, "If you are going to come after me, come after me with your whole heart and seek my face. Come embrace the heartbeat of God." Those words burned in me and touched my heart. The fear of the Lord fell heavily on me as I communed with the Spirit. The bishop called my name out, and that brought me out of the Spirit. He had realized something was going on with me. He said, "I didn't know where she was, but she was not here with us! She was gone somewhere else in the Spirit."

I was still meditating on what the Spirit had told me; I was still listening to God in my soul. I smiled and asked God, "What do you mean embrace your heartbeat?" He answered, "Just as you would embrace others when you greet them and you feel their heartbeat. That's how I want you to feel my heartbeat. Get as close to me as you can because I want you to feel my heartbeat." I was to desire nothing but God's perfect will to be done in my life. I have pondered His words in my heart. I had a banner made with those words on it along with the scripture that described David as a man after God's own heart.

> And afterward they desired a king: God gave unto them Saul the son of Cis, a man of the tribe of Benjamin, by the space of forty years. And when he had removed him; he raised up unto them David to be their king; to whom also he gave testimony, and said, I have found David the son of Jesse, a man after mine own heart, which shall fulfil all my will. (Acts 13:21–22 KJV)

It hangs in my church to remind me of those words.

My prayer is this.

"God, see my heart. Teach me how to discipline myself in my walk with you. Show me what to do so I will be able to feel your heartbeat and so you will get the glory out of everything I do in your name. Teach me how to be the pastor you have called me to be, a God-fearing pastor who will speak whatever you want me to speak to your people. I don't desire to be a people preacher; I desire to be a true woman of God who does not fear people but who fears you.

"Let me become the pastor and leader you have destined me to be who always stands on your Word with my spiritual ear and listens to you. Show me what to do with all you have given me. Let my life be pleasing to you."

All my encounters with God have gotten me to where I am in Jesus now and have kept me encouraged. My God is real! As the song says, "If God is dead, who can tell me where his body lies? For I know He Lives! ... He Lives! ... He Lives! ... He Lives!" I don't have to ask God anymore to let me touch Him to see if he is real because I know for sure He is from what I have encountered in life including my storms, trials, disappointments, tears, heartaches, rejections, and tests He has walked with me through. He has always lifted me despite my shortcomings. I always remembered these words whenever I felt like giving up: "Good, Better, and Best ... Never Let It Rest Until Your Good Is Better and Your Better Is Your Very Best!" God is real, and He will reign forever. That's why I can witness that there is nothing too hard for God to do for me or anybody else. He just does it on His time because He is an on-time God. His time is far better than mine; we must have patience and faith in God. As James says in James 1:4 ... (KJV): "But let patience have her perfect work, that ye may be perfect and entire, wanting nothing." The apostle Paul said in Philippians 1:6 (KJV),

[I am] ... being confident of this very thing, that he which hath begun a good work in you will perform it until the day of Jesus Christ. So, there is no need for any of us that serve the Lord with our whole heart ... just to become weary of what God can do. Or what he will do with us ... for us ... through us ... to us ... and even by us. When we do what God said for us to do then we can ask anything and believe it ... and He shall give it to us.

John 14:14 (KJV) reads, "If ye shall ask anything in my name, I will do it." I'm not hung up on having so many material things; I desire the perfect will of God in my life and to be rich in the wisdom, knowledge, and understanding of His Word.

CHAPTER 5

LEARNING HOW TO STAY FOCUSED ON JESUS

W hen we have learned to focus on Jesus, He will show us how to embrace the heartbeat of God. He'll show us how to stay in tune with all He promised to bring to pass in our lives.

I always try to surround myself with nothing but positive things and sayings that remind me where I want to go in God. A plaque in my office reads, Time Spent Waiting on God Is Never Wasted. We can learn to allow God to order our steps in His Word and not let sin have dominion over us. Psalm 117:133 (KJV) reads, "Order my steps in thy word and let not any iniquity have dominion over me. We can make this journey victoriously." When I become discouraged or afraid, God reminds me of Psalm 37:1–2 (KJV): "Fret not thyself (Don't get scared). Neither be thou envious against the workers of iniquity (Don't be jealous or become a backstabber). For they shall soon be cut down like the grass and wither as the green herb (They will be exposed and brought low like the grass)."

If we learn to rest in the Lord, we will be confident He will come through for us and we'll be able to slay every giant that comes against us. We will overcome all witches and warlocks who try to stop our progress in the Lord if we pray God's Word back to them. We must study His Word and embed some scriptures in our spiritual bellies. When troubles come and storms rise up in our lives, we will conquer them with our inner spiritual vocabulary, pray with the Word of God, and be assured He will come to our rescue.

You will embrace the heartbeat of God when you can pray, "God, you said that if I put my trust in you, I would never be ashamed. You said that in times of trouble, you would be right there. You said that you would give me whatever I ask for in faith and doubt not in my heart."

Learn scriptures such as these.

> No weapon that is formed against thee shall prosper; and every tongue that shall rise against thee in judgement thou shall condemn. This is the heritage of the servants of the Lord, and their righteousness is of me, saith the Lord. (Isaiah 54:17 KJV)

> The steps of a good man are ordered by the Lord; and he delighteth in his way. (Psalm 37:23)

Order my steps in thy word and let not any iniquity
have dominion over me. (Psalm 119:133 KJV)

For the Lord God is a sun and shield: the Lord will
give grace and glory: no good thing will he withhold
from them that walk uprightly. (Psalm 84:11 KJV)

Our spiritual bellies need to be fed with God's Word so we will
become palm tree Christians who spring back after the storms of
life have knocked us down. We will be able to bring forth the Word
in us and show others its power and authority. It will come alive, rise
up in us, and bring us back to life in Him. If we feed ourselves God's
Word, we will grow spiritually and understand what it is saying to
us individually and collectively. His Word is our shield and buckler
in our spiritual warfare; it speaks life to dying and helpless souls.
Understanding what God is saying to us through His Word will
give us the authority to use it when we face our enemies. We will
be able to say it with confidence and walk in it with assurance that
God said it. We will confuse our enemies, and what we declare,
decree, and command will come to pass. God said that, and we
should believe that.

If we feed our souls and spirits with the Word of God, we will
become healthy saints of God. Daniel and his three friends became
spiritually healthy by refusing the king's meal: "But Daniel purposed
in his heart that he would not defile himself with the portion of
the king's meat, nor with the wine which he drank: therefore he
requested of the prince of the eunuchs that he might not defile

himself" (Daniel 1:8 KJV). By refusing to eat the king's meat, they were able to pull down the strongholds that would have destroyed them. Let us not eat every word given to us before we are sure it is sound doctrine coming from God's Word!

Learn to Embrace God's Heartbeat

We will surely and effectively know how to embrace one another in the Spirit when we learn to embrace the heartbeat of God. We will love one another unconditionally with that agape love Jesus talked about in His Word. We will not look for anything back when we help one another. We will become real servants of God and spread His love to others when we let ourselves be caught up with the genuine love of Jesus.

Embrace the heartbeat of God—five powerful words. We must be hungry for His Word and presence in our lives even if we are left out on some things. It's okay for us not to fit in with the in crowd. We must stay focused on Jesus, not on worldly things, some of which we will have to lay aside. We might have to walk away from some longtime buddies and even some family members. We will have to allow God to prepare us for that kind of embracing. He must be our priority in everything.

God wants you to be completely ready to go where He plans to take you. Not everybody will be able to go with you because not everybody will be prepared or qualified to do that. You must be willing to walk with just Jesus by your faith and let God order your steps. You will be criticized because you have left a lot of things and some familiar people behind, but you will realize you are different for your own good and God's glory. You won't want to keep the same company anymore. T. D. Jakes once said that partaking in God's Spirit required a separation from worldly things. You have to learn when to separate yourself from some lifetime friends and others so you can get as close to God's bosom as possible and feel His breath.

No more business as usual. No more friendship or entertaining as usual. You have to think with a one-track mind that is focused on God alone, not on anything else. You will have some sleepless nights and face others' rejection as you seek His face. Psalm 91:1 (KJV) reads, "He that dwelleth in the secret place in the most High shall abide under the shadow of the Almighty." In that secret place, God will protect you with His blood from your enemies—those who want you to believe they are all for you while all the time they are against you. They are jealous of you because they saw God manifesting Himself in you; they see you leaving from one place in God to a place that is higher than where they are. That's why they have become distant from you. You didn't realize that until God began to take you back to the different encounters He walked you through, especially those that made you walk through the valley of the shadow of death.

You will realize how close you were to God then as He carried you through it all. You will see how He directed you in everything you had to do and go through. You will realize He had anointed everything with His blessed oil, the Great Physician's medicine. Every day, he anointed you with His sanctifying oil. His Word kept your mind focused on Jesus so that even when you felt half-dead, you whispered prayers from the depths of your soul.

My prayers carried me through all I had to face, and sometimes, my prayer was a simple "Breathe on Me, Lord!" when I had no breath to say anything else. The Lord kept His hands on me and reminded me that I had been to that place before with Him; I had embraced His heartbeat but didn't know I had.

Pastor Annie S. Blackwell

Recognizing God's Embrace in My Life

The Spirit showed me when I had embraced the heartbeat of God; the Spirit said, "Remember the day when you were sitting on the side of that ditch after you had finished supper and cleaned up the dishes. You took your Bible outdoors and read Matthew 17:14–21 concerning the healing of the demoniac boy. You begin to feel something moving underneath your skirt, and you brushed it away and kept on reading. You felt it again, but you crossed your legs and kept on reading. But as you got to the top of the next page in the Bible to verse 21, 'Howbeit this kind goeth not out but by prayer and fasting.' Look down and behold the snake crawling down your leg." You froze as you looked at a snake about twelve inches long crawl down your leg into the ditch to the water. Later on, you learned that It was a water moccasin, and all you could say was, 'Oooooh!' You heard a thump on the ground beside you, but you never looked around to see what it was. You just kept right on reading and then dosed off to sleep.

"Your son woke you up to ask you for the last piece of chicken left over from supper. You told him yes, but he looked down and said, 'Mom, don't move. There's a black snake lying beside you.' You told him, 'If you don't stop playing with that rubber snake, I'll give you a beating!' He said, 'Mom, I'm not playing. It's a real snake! Be still. I'll get the shovel.'

"Again, you froze as it got closer to you. You were scared to move. Your son came running back with the shovel. The snake moved a little ways from underneath you. I guess he had lifted his head up. You hoped your son didn't miss the snake's head. You closed your eyes and heard the shovel hit the ground. Your son killed the snake. I was walking with you then.

"During all the bad times you have been through, you held onto me though you didn't understand it then. But you never gave up. Yes, you made some bad choices, but you never gave up on me. David said in Psalm 42:1–4, 'As the hart panteth after the water brooks, so panteth my soul after thee, O God. My soul thirsteth for God, for the living God: when shall I come and appear before God?'

"I saw you running for your life. I saw you seeking refuge for your soul. I heard you crying out of your heart. Just like David, I heard you crying out from the depths of your soul. As Maschil, the chief musician, wrote for the sons of Korah in Psalm 42:3, 'My tears have been my meat day and night, while they continually say unto me, Where is your God?' When you remembered what you chose to let go of to save your marriage and family, I was drawing you closer to me, but you didn't know it because you were full of pain, hurt, and anguish. You poured out your soul to me, but it seemed to you that I was far away. Nonetheless, I was still there waiting for you to talk to me.

"You found no rest or comfort. Still, you didn't give up on me. You kept seeking my face for help. One time, you sheltered twenty-three family members in your home, and every evening, you all had to go to the church. I instructed you how to go through this spiritual warfare with the demons surrounding your home. Chaos was all around you, but you still kept pressing your way to church for my help looking for answers you could not find. You were seeking my heartbeat then, but you didn't know I was molding you then."

I Was There All the Time

"I even showed you my glory during a revival you were running. My glory came over that revival like a fog. It started from the back of the church and moved to the front. It was slaying people in the Spirit. They ran to the altar and cried out to me. You saw my glory, but you didn't recognize it.

"My child, I have been with you since you first gave your life to me. I have always had my hands on you. I found favor with you because of your zeal when you first were saved. Do you remember in the fall of 2015 the day you had made some homemade rolls and you turned the oven on? You went into the living room to wait for the oven to get hot. About thirty minutes later, you checked the oven, but it was cold. When you opened the door, the pilot light made that *poof* sound to come on, but there was no heat.

"You turned the oven up to 450 degrees still not realizing something had to be wrong with the oven. You went back to the living room. About twenty minutes later, someone said he smelled gas. By that time, everybody in the house smelled it. You ran back to the kitchen to check the oven. You opened the oven without even thinking that was the wrong thing to do. It could have exploded, but I was there in the midst of that flame in that oven. The pilot light had come on, and the oven was filled with gas. That was me. I held back death so you and your family would have life.

"Remember when you developed fluid and an infection in the lining of your heart; it hurt you to even breathe. You had to sit up with four pillows and a booster behind you to breathe, but breathing hurt. You didn't know it then, but you had reached that place in me.

"You had embraced my heartbeat before all of these things had happened to you. That's why you were able to go through them and they didn't take you out of here. You had sought me in the midnight hours alone and fasted and prayed for such things as these.

"I brought you to my secret place, where you rested in my arms under the shadow of my wings. You had submitted and committed your will to mine. My desires became yours. I granted what you desired for my glory and name's sake. You were seeking my face and my will. That is where I want you to meet me again. Material things didn't really matter to you anymore, but I gave them to you anyway because you focused on what pleased me."

Life is beautiful when God is in our lives. We are all creating our legacies every day God allows us to live, and we should always remember that. Someone may be sitting in front of our casket or our sickbed trying to comfort our loved ones. It will not matter what the preacher will preach at our funeral or say about us. Let us strive as John said in Revelations 14:13 (KJV): "And I heard a voice from heaven saying unto me, Write. Blessed are the dead which die in the Lord from henceforth. Yea, saith the Spirit that they may rest from their labour; and their works do follow them." John wrote in John 9:4 (KJV), "I must work the work of him that sent me, while it is day: the night cometh, when no man can work." In other words, John was saying let us work while it is day, while we are living. For when night cometh, when we die, no man can work. There is nothing else we can do beneath the grave for God. Ecclesiastes 9:5 (KJV) lets us know, "For the living know they shall die: but the dead know not anything, neither have they have any more reward; for the memory of them is forgotten."

CHAPTER 6

LISTEN TO GOD WITH YOUR SPIRITUAL EAR

J ohn encouraged us way back then to come after the heartbeat of God with all our might and soul so we would live righteous lives according to His Word. We shouldn't worry about how our obituaries read or what people say about us; that won't matter to God. He is concerned only with whether we have lived faithfully. Everyone will know that we knew God as our personal Savior, that we did the best we could to obey God's Word, and that God knew us as His children.

It won't matter what they write about us or how beautifully they dress us up for the casket. The only thing that will matter is if we were dressed in His righteousness and power because we had lived as true children of God and had a relationship with Him that portrayed the life of Jesus in our lives. We are to be lights to a dying world. Matthew 5:14 (KJV) reads, "Ye are the light of the world. A city that sitteth upon a hill cannot be hid."

People should see God in you and desire to follow you as you follow Jesus Christ.

Walking in the Likeness of Jesus Christ

Each day, we write a page in our book, our legacy; that's why every day God grants us and gives us more time to get it right. We ought to witness to others about God's goodness and miracles in our lives; that's the most important thing we can do for the Lord. In that way, others will see Him in us and want to be saved. We might seem peculiar to others, but that is the reflection of Christ in our lives.

We must proclaim the gospel of Jesus Christ through our acts and deeds and let God's Word become alive in our life and through it. The most effective way for us to become partakers of His crucifixion is to become examples of the way He lived on earth. We embrace God's heartbeat when we desire to be more like Him than anything else.

We should let Jesus's love come alive in, through, for, with, to, and by us in the way we walk and talk and how we treat one another including strangers and the unsaved. Hebrews 13:1–2 (KJV) reads, "Let brotherly love continue. Be not forgetful to entertain strangers for some have entertained angels unawares." If we want to embrace God's heartbeat, we must create a sincere relationship with Him and allow Him to show, lead, and guide us in His ways so we can fulfill His perfect will and purpose for our lives. Jeremiah 29:12–13 (KJV) lets us know how we can seek to embrace God's heartbeat: "Then shall ye call upon me, and ye shall go and pray unto me, and I hearken unto you. And ye shall seek me, and find me when ye shall search for me with all of your heart."

Another way we can embrace the heartbeat of God is to be honest with Him and man and let His love order all our footsteps. At times, God will want us to be alone with Him. Desiring to embrace God's heartbeat carries a great responsibility and purpose; there is a great price to pay in seeking His heartbeat, and it could include suffering without a cause for Christ's sake. The apostle Paul said in Romans 8:18 (KJV) something that has been one of my favorite scriptures during my sickness: "For I reckon that the suffering of this present time, can not be compared with the glory that shall be revealed in us." It will cost a lot of meditation on and study of God's Word, a lot of fasting and agonizing prayer and consecration. We will have to commune with God alone more than anyone else and most of all let the Spirit lead our thoughts, paths, and especially our mouths. Our spiritual ears should be sensitive to God's voice, and our spiritual vision should be focused on Jesus.

When we pray, we should always desire that our prayers reach God's ear and that He will thus wake up heaven for us. I thought about Stephen's stoning in Acts 7: 54, 60 when someone knocked his eye out with a stone. I imagine Jesus saying, "Father, forgive them for they know not what they do."

I'm not saying we have to walk around like zombies not paying attention to what is around us. I am saying we have to discipline ourselves in all things—our ways, talk, and habits and the people we hang with, who should be spiritually minded people. We have to pray always for the Spirit's guidance, live by God's Word, and discerning what is right and what is wrong. We must know our hearts. These are all ways we can please God and show our fear of Him. We should be careful for nothing but in everything by prayer and supplication with thanksgiving let our requests be made known unto God.

The apostle Paul spoke about the Word of God in Philippians 4:6. Before doing or saying something, ask yourself if it will glorify God and His Word. Always have your spiritual ear tuned to God's voice. Every day, I want Jesus Christ walking with me so I will reflect Him to others and shift the atmosphere as Jesus did as He traveled on earth.

When I felt I was all alone, He came just as it was with Moses every time he went into God's presence. God's glory was shining on him when he returned to the children of Israel, and they knew he had been talking with God. I have had the privilege of seeing God's anointing on others. That's why I know God is the same yesterday, today, and forever. He will do for us what He did for others way back then.

Allow God to direct your whole being. Let the Word follow your life as Jesus said it would: "Signs following Believers." Signs of His coming are everywhere you look. His presence is more real in the atmosphere than ever. Jesus is on his way back, and that's no joke. If you are a student of the Bible, you will agree with me. I pray that this book will enlighten you on the reality of Jesus as your Savior. God is not dead. He's alive in all of us. If you are not saved, I pray that something in this book has caught your attention and that you consider giving your life to Jesus, who died for our sins.

We must choose between heaven and hell. Good people don't necessarily go to heaven. Matthew 5:8 (KJV) reads, "Blessed are the pure in heart: for they shall see God." Only the righteous will see God. Those with good intentions, those who go to church, those who tithe generously, will not necessarily make it to heaven.

We will end up in one place or the other, and God will not go against our will if we desire to serve the devil (Joshua 24:13–27). He gave His life so we could receive salvation through His blood.

Where do you want to spend eternity?

God Has a Shield of Protection around You

When you begin to draw close to God, He will draw close to you and begin to reveal Himself to you in special and unique ways. He will open up your understanding of His wisdom and knowledge concerning His will for your life.

That is where I want to be in Him again. My mind goes back to the time that God had to walk me through the leukemia my first husband had. I had to stay focused and seek God's face. Even before that, I knew God was drawing me into His presence though I didn't understood where I was in God then or what would happen in my life. But I began to feel a special touch and closeness with God. He reminded me that those were the times that I had embraced His heartbeat. He told me this.

"But you didn't know that you had been to that place before with me. Do you remember in 1982 when you went to Tampa to bring your mother back to live with you and your family? She was sick with no one to attend to her. On your way back when you were near South Carolina, you took the wheel from your brother to finish the trip. He soon fell asleep after having driven such a long way. Nobody was awake but you and your mom, who talked to you so you would stay awake. You said with confidence, 'And His mercy endureth forever.' It seemed an evil force had taken hold of the steering wheel. It sounded like a tire had blown. The car was snatched around backward by an evil force, and you were going sixty-five miles per hour backward. It was as if the steering wheel had locked up on you.

All you could do was hold it. That evil force, whatever it was, was pulling the car backward down the road into the swamp."

All I could do was close my eyes and wait to hear the bang and the boom I knew I would hear on impact. As we were going down the bank of the road, my life flashed before me. I was sure the car would blow up as it settled in that swamp. But God's hands were on us. His favor on my life made old death behave. God didn't let the car go completely into the swamp, only halfway. That all happened as my brother, my husband, and my two little children were asleep in the back seat. They woke up only when my mom screamed and they felt the car hit a tree in the swamp. They woke up asking, "What's happening?"

The car was steaming because the motor was hot and in the water. I said, "Everybody stay calm," but my mom was screaming and desperately trying to get out of that car; the passenger side was in that swamp.

I didn't think of it then, but my mom used a walker. She, however, forgot all about that at that moment. She stood up somehow on the seat and yelled at me to get out of her way and let her out of that car. I guess I was panicking; I didn't move. I was waiting for the car to explode. I was sure we would die.

We all got out and walked up the bank to the road. Drivers who had seen us sliding down to the swamp backward had stopped. We were unharmed and they told us that we had been lucky. They had seen how fast we had been going, and they had heard the boom when we hit that tree even from across the road. Not another car was coming on our side of the road; it was as if God had stopped all the traffic farther back. I told them that we had not been lucky; we had avoided injury due to God's mercy and grace.

I wondered how we would get home. We waited for the tow truck. When it came, it pulled the car out of the swamp. To our surprise, none of the tires had blown. We drove home on the one we had thought had blown. We saw black skid marks on the road a good hundred and fifty feet or more. There was only a little dent in the side of the car from smashing against the tree that stopped us from going any deeper in that swamp.

I knew God's great hands had held that car up in that swamp, and I know of many times when God stopped the hand of death in my life and protected me from my enemies with His grace and mercy. One time, the devil tried to take me out with someone who tried working witchcraft on me, but God wouldn't let anything happen to me. In fact, He showed me the individual in a dream. But I never breathed a word to anyone about that; I just watched God move on my behalf. I thought, *Okay, God. I've felt your heartbeat before.*

Some who read this book won't believe it, but that's because they're spiritually blind concerning God's power in our lives. None of this book is made up; God showed up in my life many times including that time when He warned me about the witchcraft.

One day, I was in the kitchen preparing supper, and my little granddaughter was sitting at the table watching me. As I began to go from the stove to the sink, the Spirit said, "Look down on the floor in front of you." A baby snake was coming out the door under the sink. I stopped, and my granddaughter screamed, "Look, Granny! A snake!" The Spirit told me, "There is death in the house!" I thought that because it was a little snake, it meant it would be my little granddaughter. I didn't say anything to anyone because the snake disappeared just that fast. I opened the doors to the sink, but I never saw the snake again.

I never thought of it again until my husband had passed; the Lord brought it back to my memory. Now I understood the sign of that snake: it was going to be my husband taken away from us. At times after my husband had passed, I heard God knock on my door. I was home by myself one early morning when I heard a knock. I went to the door to see who it was, but nobody was there. I went back in the kitchen and stood by the sink. I began to cry about my first husband's passing, and I felt God's presence in the kitchen. He stood beside me, and I rested my head on His bosom as He held me close. I felt comfort in His body and presence. I knew it was God by the way He embraced me; He had some height to Him. That always happened when I was home alone. Sometimes, I would start to cry and God's presence would fill the house.

Whenever my heart felt so lonely, God was there even at times when I felt like giving up on myself. When I would slip and fall from where I was with God, I would hear Him call me by my name with anger in His voice: "You know better!"

Fear filled my heart. For a little while, I was scared to live by myself. I would dread nighttime. He was always coming to me in dreams and visions trying to get my attention, but I was angry with God and didn't want to listen to Him. However, God did just what He had promised me—He would never leave me alone or forsake me. I cannot explain it, but God wouldn't let me go. I have felt God's embrace at times I needed His assurance.

I often think of the times in my life when I saw God moving things out of my way; I didn't have to do anything other than what God told me to do: "Be still and know that I am God. Be still and see the work of the Lord! Watch me work a work within a work on your behalf!" I long to be in the center of His will and discern things about myself and others before they ever happen. God would even show me those who were against me because I had prayed for Him to do that, and I learned who they were and how to pray for them.

Obeying God will carry you to that secret place in Him as David mentioned in Psalm 91:1–2. I'm not talking about what somebody else has told me; I'm talking about what I have personally experienced. God deals with all of us according to our faith and our faithfulness to Him, and I knew exactly where I was in God at that time.

If we want to embrace God's heartbeat, we must seek that faithfully, persistently, and consistently in our fasting and prayer life. We can commune with God in the midnight hours when everybody else is sleeping. We must develop a stable atmosphere around us so we can stand firm in God. What an awesome experience we can have with God if we are attentive to what He shows or directs us to do and submit to His will for us.

Having Confidence in the Most High God

Even if nobody believes in you or understands you, keep your eyes fastened on Jesus. Embracing the heartbeat of God requires a separation from negative things and negative people. I know exactly what I need to do just as I used to—stay in consecration and meditation, and stay in that Word and in the face of God.

I let God talk to me through His Word, and I talk to Him in my prayers and my studying His Word. I have learned there is a certain sound God needs to hear from His people as they worship and pray to Him. As you are called by God, you need to learn how to stay before Him as a leader. The apostle Paul said that we were to live by what we preach and be true examples to others even if that makes us feel uncomfortable.

Luke 18:1 (KJV) reads, "Men ought to always to pray and not to faint." We are to pray without ceasing and always be forgiving. We are to love one another without jealousy or envy or holding grudges. We are to keep our hearts pure and allow the fruit of the Spirit to manifest itself in our lives. We are not to dress to bring attention to ourselves and allow the evil eye to produce works of the flesh in our lives. In Galatians 5:16–17 (KJV), we read, "This I say then Walk in the Spirit; and ye shall not fulfil the lust of the flesh. For the flesh lusteth against the Spirit, and the Spirit against the flesh: and these are contrary the one to the other: so that ye cannot do the things that ye would do."

We can never serve God in our flesh; we must seek His spirit so it will rest upon our lives. We are to walk with Him and please Him in all our ways. Last but not least, we must WATCH AND PRAY.

W: watch your Ways, the way you do and look at others.

A: watch your Actions, the way that you conduct yourself.

T: watch your Talk, you conversations with others

C: watch the Company you keep.

H: watch your Habits because habits, especially bad ones, can be hard to break.

A: have Assurance in Christ Jesus.

N: Never give up on God.

D: be Devoted in your relationship with God.

P: be Persistent in your prayers.

R: be Ready to serve others.

A: Always pray and not faint.

Y: Yield yourself totally to Jesus.

Those you associate with who cannot deposit spiritual righteousness in you will not help you in your walk with God. You need to ask God for directions for your life and whom you need to let go of. My prayer is that this book will help you open your spiritual eyes and heart to God's calling on your life. You should go after God's heartbeat and seek Him just as you would seek a loved one who has been lost for years.

He calls us to repent, but we will have to make up our own minds on that. I pray that your answer will be, "Yes Lord! Here I am. All the bad things and disappointments that came up in my life helped me prepared for the hardest storms and tests I had to go through because there was nobody I could depend on to be there for me. But God, they taught me how to put my faith in you and not in man."

I tried to go through my struggles alone, and I failed God by trying to do that in my own strength. That showed me that my life was nothing without Him in it. Others' rejection of me made me trust God all the more. My loneliness molded me into the person God wanted me to become. At that time, though, I didn't understand God was working behind the scenes of my life.

Yes, sometimes, I felt I had been thrown out as I heard my mom say with the bathwater and nobody cared or wanted me around. But God uses our troubles to mold us; my troubles unsettled me and led me to become established in the Word of God, seek Him, and depend on Him. I learned that God is always as close as the mention of His name—Jesus!

Trials come only to make us stronger in the Lord: "The Lord hears the cry of His people and He will attend to their supplication." Psalm 37:6 (KJV) reads, "Many are the afflictions of the righteous but the Lord will deliver them out of them all."

What a relief and consolation to know that there is power and strength in the Word of God. What other words can be uttered with such strength in them? It will lift and strengthen your spirit and give you hope when you thought all hope was gone. If it had not been for the Lord on my side, my enemies would have swallowed me up! The Lord is my shepherd, and I shall not want. I know that if I wait on the Lord, He will strengthen my heart. Hallelujah! What great words to have birthing out of your spiritual belly!

Here are more comforting words: If God be for me, He is more than the whole world against me. My God is my strong tower and a shelter in the time of my storms! He's my help in the very present time of trouble. No weapon formed against me shall prosper. Such words feed your soul and put life back into you. Psalm 42:1 (KJV) reads, "As the hart panteth after the water brook. My soul panteth after God."

There will come a time when the enemy will try to kill you. That will be the time when you have to run as fast as you can to God. It's good to know the Lord before trouble comes as King David did when his enemies were after him. You don't have to faint or give up; just say as David said in Psalm 121:1–2 (KJV), "I will look unto the hills from whence cometh my help. My help cometh from the Lord, who made heaven and earth."

We must be sure we are in a right relationship with God to be confident He will deliver us from our enemies. He can deliver us from a double-minded state and help us live righteous lives. I feel such a calmness in my spirit with the blessed assurance that God will show up just when I need Him the most. I have walked in my integrity toward God in all my ways to the best of my ability, and my Redeemer lives in me; that's why I can call on Him and He will come to my rescue.

I'm not saying we won't have to suffer, But as Peter said in 1 Pet. 5:10 (KJV), "But the God of all grace, who hath called us unto his eternal glory by Christ Jesus, after that ye have suffered a while, make you perfect, stablish, strengthen, settle you."

As I get older, I don't worry about the things I never had in this life; I focus more on seeing Jesus and living eternally in the house of the Lord. My former pastor used to say that he wanted his last days to be his best days knowing he had fought a good fight in the Lord. That was not because the apostle Paul had written that but because in your last days, you will want to know you have done your best to live for God.

I'm not worried about what I have missed out on down here. I'm not moving too fast; I'm just trying to make sure that when I see Jesus, He will be pleased to meet me, and I will sure enough be overwhelmed to embrace Him face to face. I will hear Him say to me, "Well done, my daughter, thou good and faithful servant. You have been faithful over a few things. All that I placed in your hands you have kept, and nothing was plucked out of your hands by the devil. Come on up and I'll make you ruler over many. Welcome home, my daughter!" I will thank God because I made it over the line!

Know for Sure That We Are of God

Lord, my prayer is that we as your people will walk close to you and after you as we walk among the unsaved. They will see you in us and desire to follow us as we follow you. In Jesus's name, let the redeemed of the Lord say amen! It is so because God said so and I believe it.

I pray that this book will help you decide to give your life completely to Jesus, stretch your faith, and try Jesus for yourself. Understand that it doesn't matter how good a life you have lived, or how much money you have, how much material stuff you have accumulated in this life, or how well known you were among other people. What really matters is this. Did you include Jesus in your life? Did you know Jesus as your personal Savior? Was Jesus your first priority? Can Jesus call you His friend as He called Abraham and His disciples? That was because Jesus knew them and they had walked with Jesus themselves. As one of my favorite songs that I love to sing "All of my Life, I say Yes Lord."

I understand now that all I have endured was for my good and meant to draw me closer to God. I must work while it is day, while I still have life in my body. For when night cometh—that is, when I die—I will not be able to work anymore.

Oh how I long to embrace God's heartbeat again! How I long to reach that place in Him again! Lord, take me there to that higher place, to that secret place of yours, so I can stay in your presence with you. Remember this, a little poem that just came up in my spirit.

As I labor down here just to see my Savior face to
face,
I pray that when I meet Him, we'll enjoy each other's
embrace.
And as I look back over my life and see all that I've
come through,
I'll be able to say, "Lord, I came through all just
because of you!"
And as I go before the Lord, there I will stand,
But thank God I won't hear Him say,
"Because you did preach what I told you to preach;
The people's blood was not found on this preacher's
hand."

All my heartaches, disappointments, rejections, scorning, being
talked about, being disbelieved, overlooked, ignored, and being
cast aside are the kinds of things that have pushed me to where I
am in God today. Those are the kinds of things God used to make
me stronger in my faith and in my love for Him. So I can thank all
my haters and all those who disliked me. I'm not saying that in a
negative way because I now understand why I had to go through
what I went through. God sometimes uses ordinary people to push
us where we need to go and to be in Him and reach His goals for all
of us. We will have to pay a high price for the privilege of embracing
the heartbeat of God, but we will then have His blessed anointing
to rest in and on in our lives. The price we will have to pay is being

completely sold out to God and knowing we have sold ourselves out to Him completely.

I am learning how to suffer knowing that if I suffer with Him, one day, as the apostle Paul told us, I will reign with Him and I'll gain eternal life. I long for the day when I can see Him face to face. As the apostle Paul said, let us go on to perfection (maturity) in Christ Jesus. Let us press to the higher calling, which is in Christ Jesus.

May the Lord bless you very well through the ministering of this book. And may God open your spiritual eyes and your spiritual heart as you walk through my life in this story. There is no fantasy in this book at all; it is a true confession of my life. I thank God for everything I had to go through. I have gained through that the mind-set, determination, and the maturity in Him that it left me with. It was worth it all.

Being a pastor, I am learning even more now. I am learning how to keep my spiritual ear tuned to the sound of God's voice. One of the things I do know is very essential to any pastor and congregation is simply this—the importance of going after God's heartbeat. I realize that I must stay before God with a deep press and determination in the heart. I know that there is never enough of God that we can contain that we will not still hunger and thirst after Him. My experience as a pastor has taken me into a deeper realm of seeking God's face.

You will discover for yourself that there is a place in God that you need to get to in order to be able to lead His people down the straight and narrow way, His way. I know for myself through all my encounters with God that there is a height in God that we can all achieve if we are His children. We can never settle for where we are in God right now no matter how high we might think we are in that regard or no matter how much we might think we know about God. There is always room for improvement in our walk with Jesus. David talks about that kind of place in Psalm 91:1 (KJV): "He that dwelleth in the secret place of the Lord."

There is a place in God that He will open up to you when He sees and knows that you are ready to walk into that place in Him. That will cause you to be separated from and walk away from the world completely. Are you ready to yield your whole self to God's will for your life? The closer you get to God, the more you will become hungry for His guidance and leading for your life and for His presence to surround you. That is where the partition from everything and everybody begins. You are now ready and willing to be used by the Master because you are completely sold out to God and are ready to become spiritually naked before Him.

Allow Him to dress you up in all of His righteousness. Come now—let us walk in the Spirit by the same rule and minding the same things.

May God's hands rest on you so you will find favor with Him.

—Pastor Annie S. Blackwell, aka Pastor Shirley Blackwell